AMERICA UNITED

IN GOD WE MUST TRUST

HAMP LEE III

(com)mission
PUBLISHING

All scripture quotations are taken from the World English
Bible.

America United: In God We Must Trust
Hamp Lee III—1st ed.

ISBN 978-1-940042-40-4

CONTENTS

*For their sakes I sanctify myself, that they
themselves also may be sanctified in truth. Not for
these only do I pray, but for those also who believe
in me through their word, that they may all be one;
even as you, Father, are in me, and I in you, that
they also may be one in us; that the world may
believe that you sent me. The glory which you have
given me, I have given to them; that they may be
one, even as we are one; I in them, and you in me,
that they may be perfected into one; that the world
may know that you sent me, and loved them, even
as you loved me.*

—John 17:19-23

INTRODUCTION

In the Pledge of Allegiance to the Flag, America is described as "one nation under God, indivisible, with liberty and justice for all." But if we look across the landscape of America, our nation is divided in many areas. The color of a person's skin, socioeconomic status, personal agendas, religious beliefs, and other discriminating factors have divided many Americans.

However, I do believe our issues in America run much deeper than black or white, rich or poor, privileged or underprivileged. Our issues culminate in an unwillingness to be an indivisible nation under God; a nation whose God is the Lord.[1]

America is in desperate need of God. Only in Him can we find the solutions to our nation's greatest ills. He is the one who can forgive our sin and heal our land.

America United: In God We Must Trust provides a perspective for resolving our nation's current condition. This book will address how we, as the church, can come together and lead America as one nation under God, indivisible, with liberty and justice for all.

DIVIDED

Then one possessed by a demon, blind and mute, was brought to him and he healed him, so that the blind and mute man both spoke and saw. All the multitudes were amazed, and said, "Can this be the son of David?" But when the Pharisees heard it, they said, "This man does not cast out demons, except by Beelzebub, the prince of the demons." Knowing their thoughts, Jesus said to them, "Every kingdom divided against itself is brought to desolation, and every city or house divided against itself will not stand.

—Matthew 12:22-25

After Jesus healed a demon-possessed blind and mute man, the Pharisees said He casts out devils by Beelzebub, the prince of devils. In response, Jesus said that every kingdom divided against itself is brought to desolation and every city or house divided against itself will not stand.

America has been divided on many issues throughout its storied history. Experiences of discrimination, hate, and violence has been a real and painful reality for many Americans. As disheartening as these circumstances might be, they not only affect those directly impacted, they affect America as a whole.

Going back to Matthew 12, Jesus said that every city or house divided against itself will not stand and every kingdom divided against itself would be brought to desolation. The division within a city, house, or kingdom represents individual and purposeful actions against another person or people. However, what many of these people might not realize is that their actions culminate in the fall of *their own* house, *their own* city, and the desolation of *their own* kingdom—including America.

The answer for the division in America is found in God, but it begins with each individual person. As Christians are called to love others as themselves, we can make individual and purposeful actions of love, restoration, and unity within our areas of responsibility and influence. Through our actions, we can illuminate the glory of God and bring our nation one step closer to repairing the division that exists within our borders.

SEPARATION OF CHURCH AND BELIEFS

John answered, "Master, we saw someone casting out demons in your name, and we forbade him, because he doesn't follow with us." Jesus said to him, "Don't forbid him, for he who is not against us is for us."

—Luke 9:49-50

Jesus found the disciples arguing about which of them was the greatest. Perceiving the thoughts of their hearts, He took a boy and sat him next to Himself. Jesus said, *"Whoever receives this little child in my name receives me. Whoever receives me receives him who sent me. For whoever is least among you all, this one will be great."*[2]

In response, John said that he and the disciples forbade someone from casting out demons in Jesus' name because he didn't follow Jesus with them. Jesus said not to forbid him because *"he who is not against us is for us."*

Sadly, within the body of Christ, Christians and churches have been divided over many issues.[3] They have used factors such as beliefs (excluding false teaching or sin), race, and socioeconomic status to determine whether they would associate with specific individuals or groups. Though there might be Christians who do not look like you, believe exactly as you do, or share a similar socioeconomic status, we all share one common belief in Jesus. Such discriminating factors have no place in our fellowship, as we are all members of one body:[4]

For as the body is one, and has many members, and all the members of the body, being many, are one body; so also is Christ. For in one Spirit we were all baptized into one body, whether Jews or Greeks, whether bond or free; and were all given to drink into one Spirit. For the body is not one member, but many. If the foot would say, "Because I'm not the hand, I'm not part of the body," it is not therefore not part of the body. If the ear would say, "Because I'm not the eye, I'm not part of the body," it's not therefore not part of the body. If the whole body were an eye, where would the hearing be? If the whole were hearing, where would the smelling be? But now God has set the members, each one of them, in the body, just as he desired. If they were all one member, where would the body be? But now they are many members, but one body. The eye can't tell the hand, "I have no need for you," or again the head to the feet, "I have no need for you." No, much rather, those members of the body which seem to be weaker are necessary. Those parts of the body which we think to be less honorable, on those we bestow more abundant honor; and our unpresentable parts have more abundant propriety; whereas our presentable parts have no such need. But God composed the body together, giving more abundant honor to the inferior part, that there should be no division in the body, but that the members should have the same care for one another. When one member suffers, all the members suffer with it. Or when one member is honored, all the members rejoice with it.

—1 Corinthians 12:12-26

The body of Christ does not solely represent one church, one denomination, one race, or one socioeconomic status. Across the nation and around the world, Christians are baptized in one Spirit into one body. As God composed the body, let there be no division among us.

ME THE PEOPLE

"Now there was a certain rich man, and he was clothed in purple and fine linen, living in luxury every day. A certain beggar, named Lazarus, was laid at his gate, full of sores, and desiring to be fed with the crumbs that fell from the rich man's table. Yes, even the dogs came and licked his sores. The beggar died, and he was carried away by the angels to Abraham's bosom. The rich man also died, and was buried. In Hades, he lifted up his eyes, being in torment, and saw Abraham far off, and Lazarus at his bosom. He cried and said, 'Father Abraham, have mercy on me, and send Lazarus, that he may dip the tip of his finger in water, and cool my tongue! For I am in anguish in this flame.'"But Abraham said, 'Son, remember that you, in your lifetime, received your good things, and Lazarus, in the same way, bad things. But now here he is comforted and you are in anguish. Besides all *this, between us and you there is a great gulf fixed, that those who want to pass from here to you are not able, and that no one may cross over from there to us.'"He said, 'I ask you therefore, father, that you would send him to my father's house; for I have five brothers, that he may testify to them, so they won't also come into this place of torment.'"But Abraham said to him, 'They have Moses and the prophets. Let them listen to them.' "He said, 'No, father Abraham, but if one goes to them from the dead, they will repent.'"He said to him, 'If they don't listen to Moses and the prophets, neither will they be persuaded if one rises from the dead.'"*

—Luke 16:19-31

Lazarus laid at the gate of the rich man's house to beg. As he was laid there, Lazarus might have had a disability that prevented him from moving freely on his own. Jesus identified only one desire from Lazarus: to be fed with the crumbs from the rich man's table.

In death, their roles reversed. Lazarus lived in comfort and the rich man in torment. The rich man asked Abraham if Lazarus or someone from the dead could go to his brothers to warn them for fear that they too would come to that place of torment.

Sadly, many people in the church today desire to live as this rich man. They concern themselves with the cares of this life—the desires of the flesh and eyes and the pride of life.[5] But here's the danger with these desires. Jesus says the cares of this world and the deceitfulness of riches will cause someone to become unfruitful.[6] Though they might have form of godliness, they'll be unproductive in accomplishing God's will because these cares and desires often produce an indifference toward godliness and obedience to His commands.[7]

We must all choose to live beyond the cares and desires of this life. As 1 John 2:17 says, *"The world is passing away with its lusts, but he who does God's will remains forever."*

You have an opportunity to consider the rich man's warning and change the course of your life. You can consider your ways before God and how you respond to those in need.

But when the Son of Man comes in his glory, and all the holy angels with him, then he will sit on the throne of his glory. Before him all the nations will be gathered, and he will separate them one from another, as a shepherd separates the sheep from the goats. He will set the sheep on his right hand, but the goats on the left. Then the King will tell those on his right hand, "Come, blessed of my Father, inherit the Kingdom prepared for you from the foundation of the world; for I was hungry, and you gave me food to eat. I was thirsty, and you gave me drink. I was a stranger, and you took me in. I was naked, and you clothed me. I was sick, and you visited me. I was in prison, and you came to me." Then the righteous will answer him, saying, "Lord, when did we see you hungry, and feed you; or thirsty, and give you a drink? When did we see you as a stranger, and take you in; or naked, and clothe you? When did we see you sick, or in prison, and come to you?" The King will answer them, "Most certainly I tell you, because you did it to one of the least of these my brothers, you did it to me." Then he will say also to those on the left hand, "Depart from me, you cursed, into the eternal fire which is prepared for the devil and his angels; for I was hungry, and you didn't give me food to eat; I was thirsty, and you gave me no drink; I was a stranger, and you didn't take me in; naked, and you didn't *clothe me; sick, and in prison, and you didn't visit me."* Then they will also answer, saying, *"Lord, when did we see you hungry, or thirsty, or a stranger, or naked, or sick, or in prison, and didn't help you?"* Then he will answer them, saying, *"Most certainly I tell you, because you didn't do it to one of the least of these, you didn't do it to me."* These will go away into eternal punishment, but the righteous into eternal life.*

—Matthew 25:31-46

The people on the right and left hand of Jesus didn't know how they did (or did not) give Him food, drink, clothes, or shelter or visit Him when He was sick or in prison. They didn't understand that the manner they treated one of the least of these was the manner they treated Him.

Jesus is outside *your* gate. He is without food, drink, clothing, and shelter, in prison, and sick in hospitals. He is without the basic needs that many people take for granted each day. And often because of this, and other reasons, He might be facing countless acts of discrimination, injustice, and violence.

Every person on earth is made in the image of God.[8] We were fearfully and wonderfully made for His glory and to show forth His praise upon the earth.[9] God loves us all—not just a specific race, gender, denomination, or group of people —the world. He loved us so much that He gave His one and only Son, Jesus, to save us from sin and death.[10]

As a Christian, you're commanded to love God with all your heart, soul, and mind and love your neighbor as yourself.[11] Your neighbor represents not only the person you live next to, but all people near and far. It's your opportunity to show everyone the same love, help, and support you would want in a similar situation.

Like the people on the right and left hand of Jesus, you'll one day give a personal account for your actions and behavior toward others. As you stand before Jesus, I pray He will say to you, *"Come, blessed of my Father, inherit the Kingdom prepared for you from the foundation of the world…"*

WE THE PEOPLE

If my people, who are called by my name, will humble themselves, pray, seek my face, and turn from their wicked ways; then I will hear from heaven, will forgive their sin, and will heal their land.

—2 Chronicles 7:14

After Solomon completed the house of the Lord and the king's house, the Lord appeared to him at night. He told Solomon that He heard his prayer and chosen that place for Himself as a house of sacrifice. The Lord said that when He shuts up the heavens so there is no rain, commands locusts to devour the land, or sends pestilence among His people, *"if my people, who are called by my name, will humble themselves, pray, seek my face, and turn from their wicked ways; then I will hear from heaven, forgive their sin, and heal their land."*

Though the Lord is specifically addressing the people of Israel, there's a principle we can learn from 2 Chronicles 7. In similar situations identified in the Bible, there have been times when a person or people petitioned the Lord to turn from pending destruction or to request His deliverance.[12]

If we can come together on one accord, we too can petition the Lord for the deliverance, restoration, and peace of our country. Using the information from 2 Chronicles 7:14, the following pages address one of the ways we can turn to the Lord on behalf of America and her citizens:

1. *If my people, who are called by my name...*

God identified the people who would seek Him: His people, who are called by His name. For us today, this would encompass the millions of Americans who identify themselves as Christians.[13]

Even as he chose us in him before the foundation of the world, that we would be holy and without defect before him in love; having predestined us for adoption as children through

*Jesus Christ to himself, according to the good
pleasure of his desire.*

—Ephesians 1:4-6

2. ...*will humble themselves*...

To humble yourself is to be brought into
subjection, to reduce self, to have (or take) a
low or modest view of your importance. With
humility, you acknowledge God's sovereignty
and rule over your life. Humility brings an
awareness of prideful and sinful acts before a
holy God. This awareness draws you toward
repentance and a recommitment or dedication
to live in a manner pleasing to God. Humility
opens your heart and mind to receive
instruction and guidance that you might not
have been willing to receive previously.

3. ...*pray*...

Prayer is communication with God. Through
prayer, you can make requests for help (for
yourself and others), provide an expression of
thanks, or use prayer as an object of
worship. Through expressions of prayer and
intercession, we can come together on behalf of
our families and friends and people across the
nation.[14]

4. *...seek My face...*

To seek God's face is to strive after, desire, or require time in His presence through prayer, praise, worship, and meditation. Psalm 24:3-6 describes four ways someone can ascend to the hill of the Lord and stand in His holy place: a person who has (1) clean hands, (2) a pure heart, (3) not lifted up his or her soul to falsehood, and (4) not sworn deceitfully.

5. *...turn from their wicked ways...*

Wickedness refers to motives and behaviors that encompass adversity, affliction, evil, and sin. Turning from wicked ways is a retreat from these motives and behaviors through repentance and godliness:

Therefore let us also, seeing we are surrounded by so great a cloud of witnesses, lay aside every weight and the sin which so easily entangles us, and let us run with patience the race that is set before us, looking to Jesus, the author and perfecter of faith, who for the joy that was set before him endured the cross, despising its shame, and has sat down at the right hand of the throne of God. For consider him who has endured such contradiction of sinners against himself, that you don't grow weary, fainting in your souls.

—Hebrews 12:1-4

Through our humility, prayer, seeking God's face, and turning from our wicked ways, the Lord can hear from heaven, forgive our sin, and heal our land. The information from 2 Chronicles 7:14 can become our response to our nation's present condition as we unify together on one accord, for one purpose— saving our great nation.

HOME SWEET HOME

What more shall I say? For the time would fail me if I told of Gideon, Barak, Samson, Jephthah, David, Samuel, and the prophets; who, through faith subdued kingdoms, worked out righteousness, obtained promises, stopped the mouths of lions, quenched the power of fire, escaped the edge of the sword, from weakness were made strong, grew mighty in war, and caused foreign armies to flee. Women received their dead by resurrection. Others were tortured, not accepting their deliverance, that they might obtain a better resurrection. Others were tried by mocking and scourging, yes, moreover by bonds and imprisonment. They were stoned. They were sawn apart. They were tempted. They were slain with the sword. They went around in sheep skins and in goat skins; being destitute, afflicted, ill-treated (of whom the world was not worthy), wandering in deserts, mountains, caves, and the holes of the earth. These all, having had testimony given to them through their faith, didn't receive the promise, God having provided some better thing concerning us, so that apart from us they should not be made perfect.

—Hebrews 11:32–40

Hebrews 11 is a testimony of the response of faith. Through a common bond of faith, men and women experienced great triumphs and victories, and others maintained a righteous testimony in spite of suffering and acts of violence such as torture, stoning, and death.

Some of the men and women listed in Hebrews 11:32–40 had to face their oppressors directly or overcome their own weaknesses through faith. Some found themselves destitute and wanderers without a home. But through faith, they obtained a testimony of a good report:

"Now faith is assurance of things hoped for, proof of things not seen. For by this, the elders obtained testimony."[15]

The assurance of what they were hoping for was the eternal city prepared for them by God.

And regardless of their experiences or circumstances, this hope was evident through the *proof* of their actions. They understood that something much better was awaiting them:

These all died in faith, not having received the promises, but having seen them and embraced them from afar, and having confessed that they were strangers and pilgrims on the earth. For those who say such things make it clear that they are seeking a country of their own. If indeed they had been thinking of that country from which they went out, they would have had enough time to return. But now they desire a better country, that is, a heavenly one. Therefore God is not ashamed of them, to be called their God, for he has prepared a city for them.[16]

As we survey the landscape of America, we witness the very best—and the very worst—of our society. And though many of us have experienced great triumphs or significant hardships and suffering, it's imperative that each of us obtains a good report in spite of our circumstances. We must set our hope on the promise to come—the assurance of entering the eternal city prepared for us. By living faithfully before God and man, you'll stand before Jesus with the assurance of receiving what you hoped for: a place prepared for you in the eternal city where no death, mourning, crying, or pain exists.[17]

America is your home today, but it's not your final resting place. While you await the blessed hope of the eternal city, live unto Jesus. Love God. Love others as yourself. Live faithfully. Let your light shine. Be a peacemaker. Strive for unity and peace among all.

CONCLUSION

As our nation is divided and in danger of desolation, we're in desperate need of intervention from God. To address the division and ills of our nation, we must place our trust and faith in God. We must exercise actions of love and godliness for all people, regardless of race, socioeconomic status, or any other discriminating factor. We must also set aside internal divisions and maintain a wholehearted commitment to unifying as one people across the nation. And together, we must humble ourselves, pray, seek God's face, and turn from our wicked ways so that God can hear from heaven, forgive our sin, and heal our land.

I pray the information contained in these pages was not only thought-provoking, but opened discussions on ways you and others can provide solutions of love and unity within your family, city, state, and nation. May you become a peacemaker who strives to bring our nation together. God bless.

ENDNOTES

1—Psalm 33:12.

2—Luke 9:48.

3—"Why are there so many different churches?" Victorious Publications, Accessed November 20, 2016, http://www.victorious.org/cbook/chur02-different-churches.

4—Proverbs 22:2, 28:4, Acts 10:34-35; Galatians 3:28; Colossians 3:11; James 2:1-9.

5—Matthew 6:24-33; 1 John 2:15-17.

6—Matthew 13:7, 22.

7—2 Timothy 3:1-5.

8—Genesis 1:27; Psalm 139:13–16.

9—Psalm 139:14; Isaiah 43:7, 21.

10—Romans 5:8; Ephesians 2:1-10.

11—Matthew 22:36-40.

12—Genesis 18:16–33; 1 Kings 21:17–29; Jonah 3:1–10.

13—"Percentage of Christians in US Drifting Down, but Still High," Gallup, Accessed November 19, 2016, http://www.gallup.com/poll/187955/percentage-christians-drifting-down-high.aspx.

14—1 Timothy 2:1-4.

15—Hebrews 11:1-2.

16—Hebrews 11:13–16.

17—John 14:1-4; Hebrews 4:1–11; Revelation 21:1–4.

(com)mission™

PUBLISHING

www.commissionpubs.com
info@commissionpubs.com